HAL•LEONARD

GUITAR PLAY•ALONG

Yuletide

VOL. 21

Tracking, mixing, and mastering by Jake Johnson
All guitars by Doug Boduch
Bass by Tom McGirr
Saxophone, Keyboards by Warren Wiegratz
Drums by Scott Schroedl

ISBN-13: 978-0-634-06214-8
ISBN-10: 0-634-06214-X

Visit Hal Leonard Online at
www.halleonard.com

HAL•LEONARD®
CORPORATION
7777 W. BLUEMOUND RD. P.O. BOX 13819
MILWAUKEE, WISCONSIN 53213

VOL. 21

Yuletide

CONTENTS

Guitar Notation Legend

THE MUSICAL STAFF shows pitches and rhythms and is divided by bar lines into measures. Pitches are named after the first seven letters of the alphabet.

TABLATURE graphically represents the guitar fingerboard. Each horizontal line represents a string, and each number represents a fret.

4th string, 2nd fret   1st & 2nd strings open, played together   open D chord

HALF-STEP BEND: Strike the note and bend up 1/2 step.

WHOLE-STEP BEND: Strike the note and bend up one step.

GRACE NOTE BEND: Strike the note and bend up as indicated. The first note does not take up any time.

SLIGHT (MICROTONE) BEND: Strike the note and bend up 1/4 step.

BEND AND RELEASE: Strike the note and bend up as indicated, then release back to the original note. Only the first note is struck.

PRE-BEND: Bend the note as indicated, then strike it.

VIBRATO: The string is vibrated by rapidly bending and releasing the note with the fretting hand.

PALM MUTING: The note is partially muted by the pick hand lightly touching the string(s) just before the bridge.

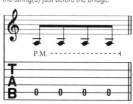

HAMMER-ON: Strike the first (lower) note with one finger, then sound the higher note (on the same string) with another finger by fretting it without picking.

PULL-OFF: Place both fingers on the notes to be sounded. Strike the first note and without picking, pull the finger off to sound the second (lower) note.

LEGATO SLIDE: Strike the first note and then slide the same fret-hand finger up or down to the second note. The second note is not struck.

SHIFT SLIDE: Same as legato slide, except the second note is struck.

TRILL: Very rapidly alternate between the notes indicated by continuously hammering on and pulling off.

TAPPING: Hammer ("tap") the fret indicated with the pick-hand index or middle finger and pull off to the note fretted by the fret hand.

NATURAL HARMONIC: Strike the note while the fret-hand lightly touches the string directly over the fret indicated.

PINCH HARMONIC: The note is fretted normally and a harmonic is produced by adding the edge of the thumb or the tip of the index finger of the pick hand to the normal pick attack.

TREMOLO PICKING: The note is picked as rapidly and continuously as possible.

VIBRATO BAR DIVE AND RETURN: The pitch of the note or chord is dropped a specified number of steps (in rhythm) then returned to the original pitch.

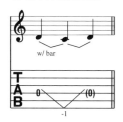

VIBRATO BAR SCOOP: Depress the bar just before striking the note, then quickly release the bar.

VIBRATO BAR DIP: Strike the note and then immediately drop a specified number of steps, then release back to the original pitch.

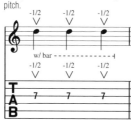

Additional Musical Definitions

 (accent) • Accentuate note (play it louder)

 (staccato) • Play the note short

D.S. al Coda • Go back to the sign (𝄋), then play until the measure marked ***"To Coda"***, then skip to the section labelled ***"Coda."***

D.C. al Fine • Go back to the beginning of the song and play until the measure marked ***"Fine"*** (end).

Fill • Label used to identify a brief melodic figure which is to be inserted into the arrangement.

N.C. • Instrument is silent (drops out).

 • Repeat measures between signs.

 • When a repeated section has different endings, play the first ending only the first time and the second ending only the second time.

5

Angels We Have Heard on High

Traditional French Carol
Translated by James Chadwick

Intro
Moderately ♩ = 100

1. An - gels we have heard on high, sweet - ly sing - ing
2. *See additional lyrics*

o'er the plains. And the moun - tains in re - ply, ech - o - ing their

joy - ous strains. Glo -

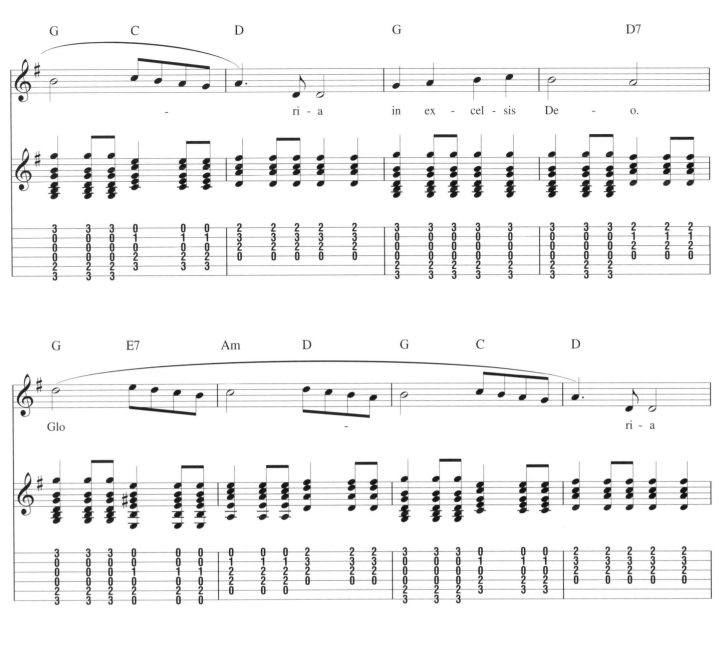

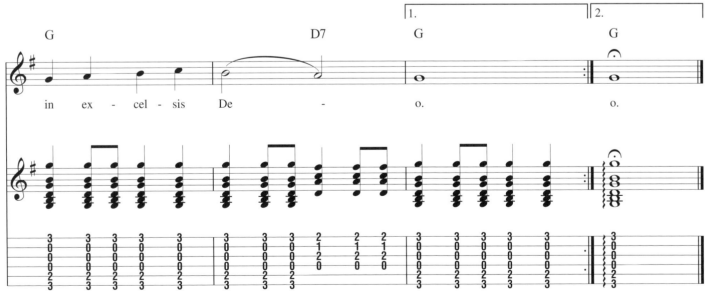

Additional Lyrics

2. Shepherds why this jubilee,
   Why your joyous strains prolong?
   What the gladsome tidings be
   Which inspire your heavenly song?

Away in a Manger

Traditional
Words by John T. McFarland (v.3)
Music by James R. Murray

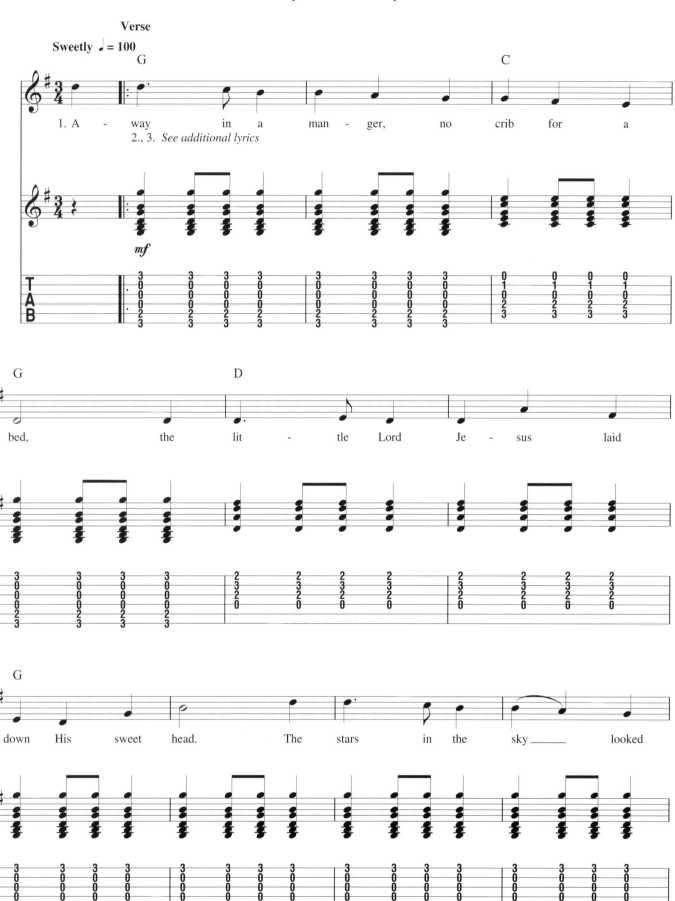

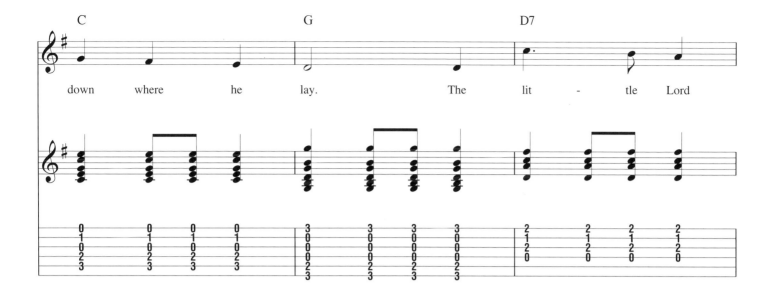

down where he lay. The lit - tle Lord

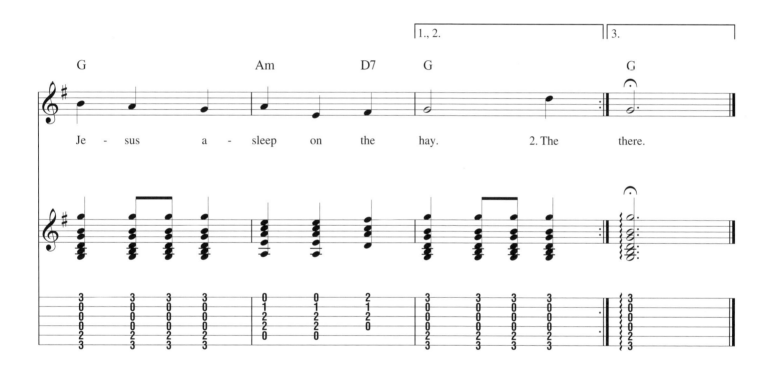

Je - sus a - sleep on the hay. 2. The there.

Additional Lyrics

2. The cattle are lowing, the baby awakes,
But little Lord Jesus, no crying He makes.
I love Thee, Lord Jesus, look down from the sky
And stay by my cradle 'til morning is nigh.

3. Be near me, Lord Jesus, I ask Thee to stay
Close by me forever and love me I pray.
Bless all the dear children in Thy tender care
And take us to heaven to live with Thee there.

Deck the Hall

Traditional Welsh Carol

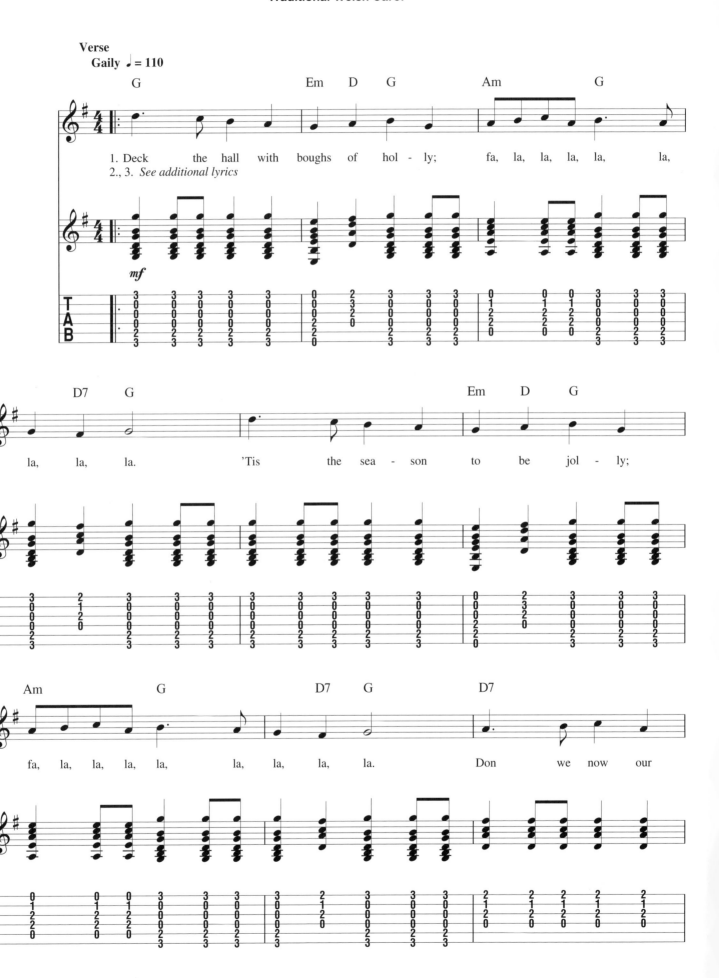

gay   ap - par - el;   fa, la, la,   la, la, la,   la, la, la.   Troll   the an - cient

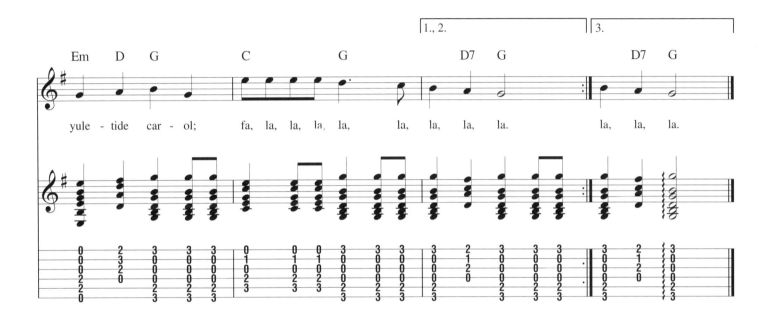

yule - tide car - ol;   fa, la, la, la, la,   la, la, la, la.   la, la, la.

Additional Lyrics

2. See the blazing yule before us;
   Fa, la, la, la, la, la, la, la, la.
   Strike the harp and join the chorus;
   Fa, la, la, la, la, la, la, la, la.
   Follow me in merry measure;
   Fa, la, la, la, la, la, la, la, la.
   While I tell of Yuletide treasure.
   Fa, la, la, la, la, la, la, la, la.

3. Fast away the old year passes;
   Fa, la, la, la, la, la, la, la, la.
   Hail the new ye lads and lasses;
   Fa, la, la, la, la, la, la, la, la.
   Sing we joyous, all together;
   Fa, la, la, la, la, la, la, la, la.
   Heedless of the wind and weather;
   Fa, la, la, la, la, la, la, la, la.

The First Noël

17th Century English Carol
Music from W. Sandys' Christmas Carols

Chorus

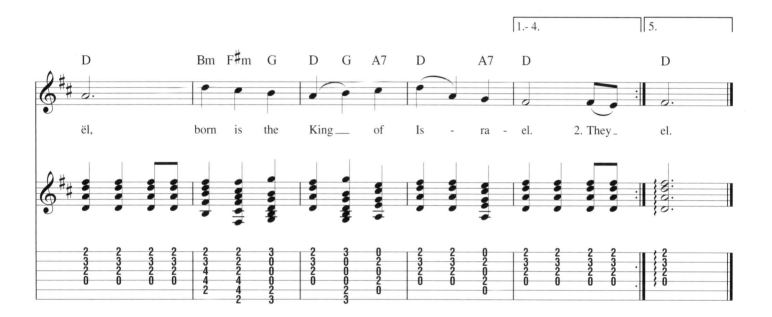

Additional Lyrics

2. They looked up and saw a star
   Shining in the East, beyond them far.
   And to the earth it gave great light
   And so it continued both day and night.

3. And by the light of that same star,
   Three wise men came from country far;
   To seek for a King was their intent,
   And to follow the star wherever it went.

4. The star drew nigh to the northwest,
   O'er Bethlehem it took it's rest;
   And there it did both stop and stay,
   Right over the place where Jesus lay.

5. Then entered in those wise men three,
   Full reverently upon their knee;
   And offered there in His presence,
   Their gold, and myrrh, and frankincense.

Go, Tell It on the Mountain

African-American Spiritual
Verses by John W. Work, Jr.

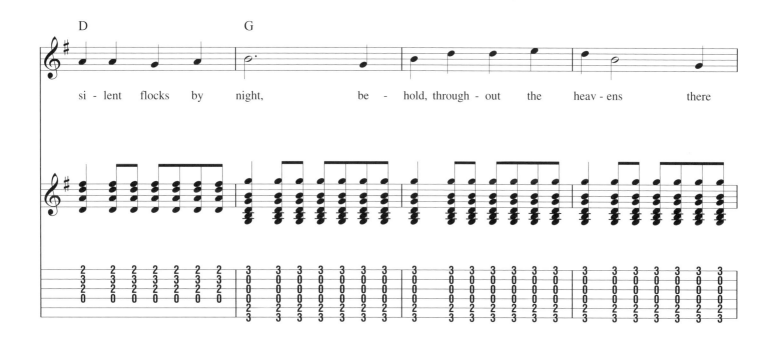

si - lent flocks by night, be - hold, through - out the heav - ens there

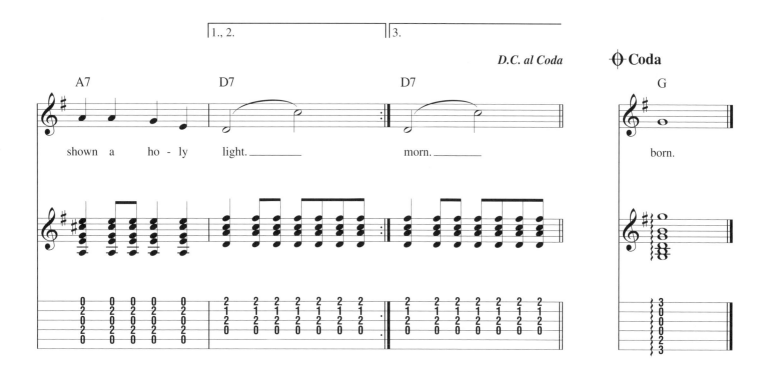

shown a ho - ly light._____ morn._____ born.

Additional Lyrics

2. The shepherds feared and trembled
   When, lo! above the earth
   Rang out the angel chorus
   That hailed our Savior's birth.

3. Down in a lowly manger
   Our humble Christ was born.
   And God sent us salvation
   That blessed Christmas morn.

Joy to the World

Words by Isaac Watts
Music by George Frideric Handel
Arranged by Lowell Mason

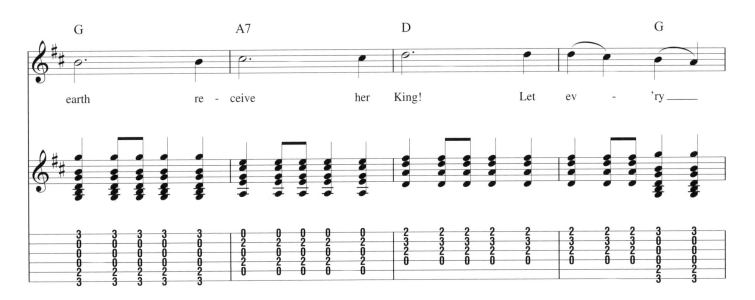

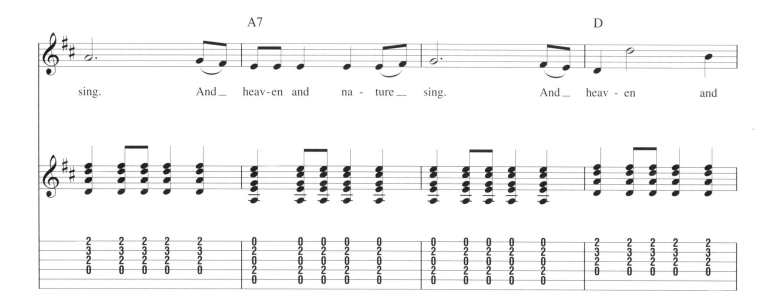

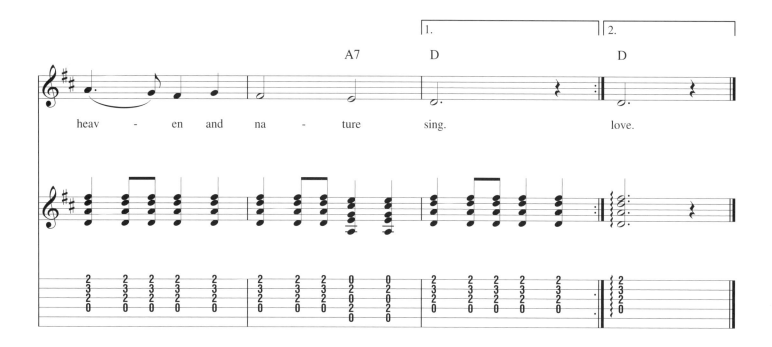

Additional Lyrics

2. He rules the world with truth and grace
   And makes the nations prove
   The glories of His righteousness
   And wonders of His love,
   And wonders of His love,
   And wonders, wonders of His love.

O Little Town of Bethlehem

Words by Phillips Brooks
Music by Lewis H. Redner

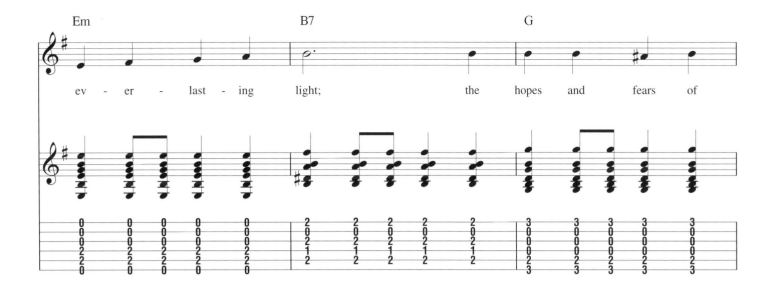

ev - er - last - ing light; the hopes and fears of

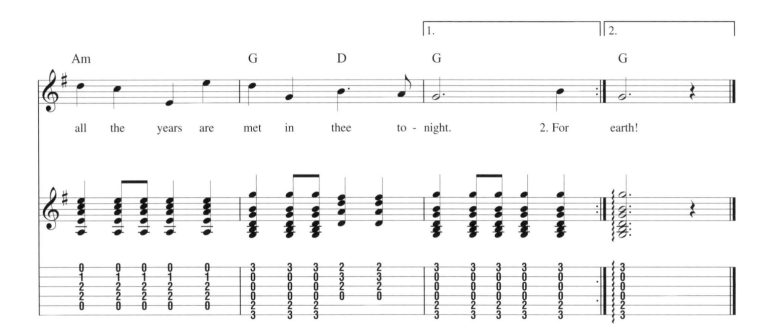

all the years are met in thee to - night. 2. For earth!

Additional Lyrics

2. For Christ is born of Mary, and gathered all above.
   While mortals sleep the angels keep
   Their watch of wond'ring love.
   O morning stars, together proclaim the holy birth!
   And praises sing to God the King,
   And peace to men on earth!

Jingle Bells

Words and Music by J. Pierpont

1. Dash - ing through the snow, in a one horse o - pen sleigh.
2., 3. *See additional lyrics*

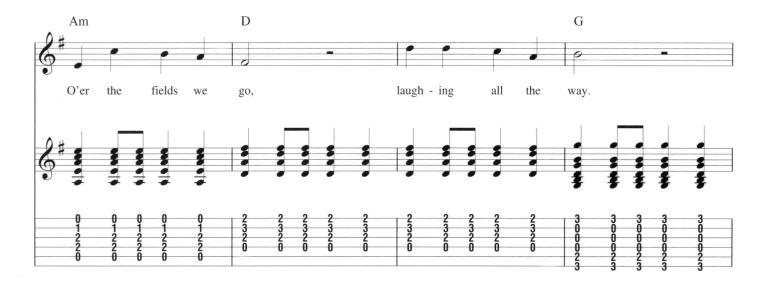

O'er the fields we go, laugh - ing all the way.

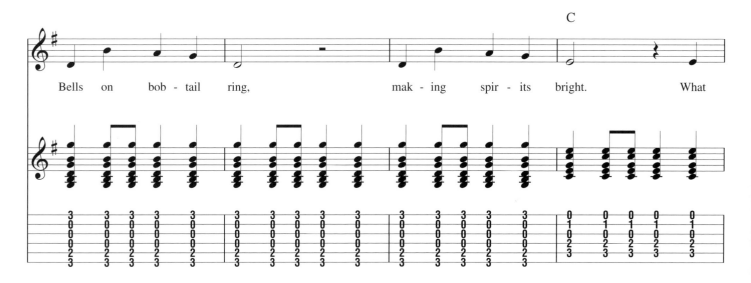

Bells on bob - tail ring, mak - ing spir - its bright. What

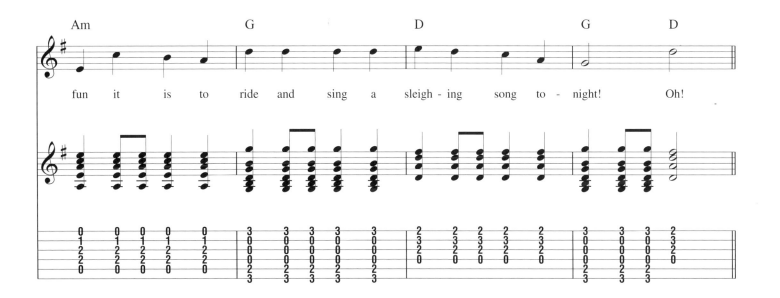

Chorus

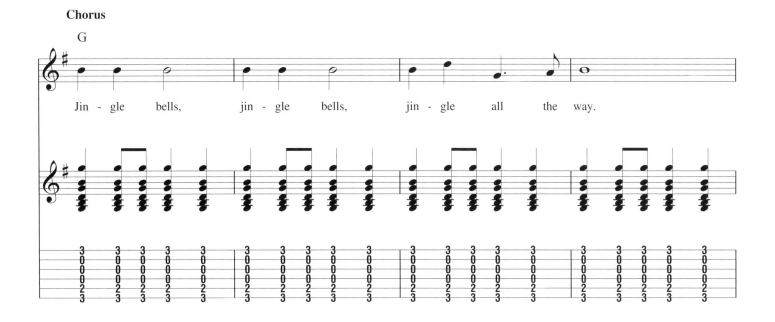

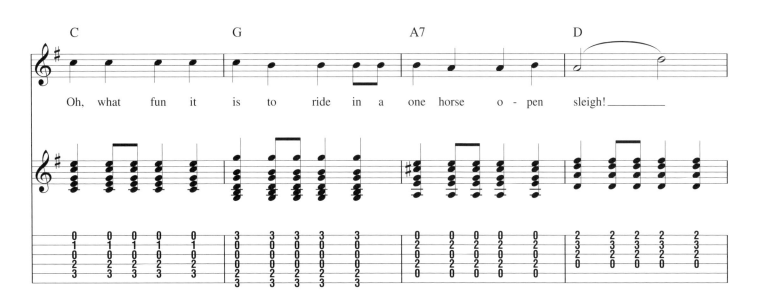

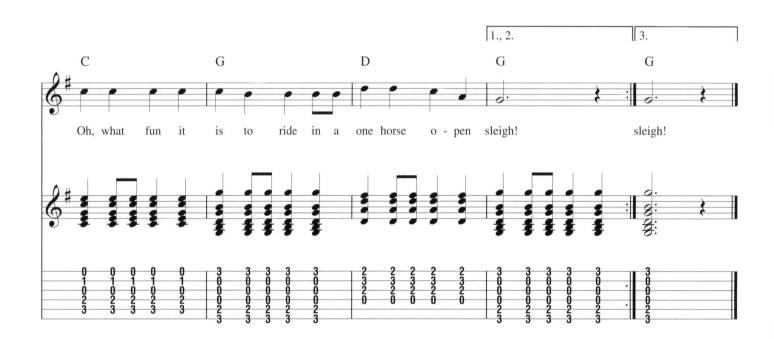

Additional Lyrics

2. A day or two ago, I thought I'd take a ride,
   And soon Miss Fannie Bright was sitting by my side.
   The horse was lean and lank,
   Misfortune seemed his lot.
   He got into a drifted bank and we, we got upshot! Oh!

3. Now the ground is white, go it while you're young.
   Take the girls tonight and sing this sleighing song.
   Just get a bobtail bay,
   Two-forty for his speed.
   Then hitch him to an open sleigh and
   Crack, you'll take the lead! Oh!

GUITAR PLAY-ALONG

INCLUDES TAB

The Guitar Play-Along Series will help you play your favorite songs quickly and easily. Just follow the tab and listen to the CD to hear how the guitar should sound, and then play along using the separate backing tracks. Mac or PC users can also slow down the tempo by using the CD in their computer. The melody and lyrics are also included in the book in case you want to sing, or to simply help you follow along. 8 songs in each book.

VOLUME 1 – ROCK GUITAR
Day Tripper • Message in a Bottle • Refugee • Shattered • Sunshine of Your Love • Takin' Care of Business • Tush • Walk This Way.
00699570 Book/CD Pack......................................$12.95

VOLUME 2 – ACOUSTIC GUITAR
Angie • Behind Blue Eyes • Best of My Love • Blackbird • Dust in the Wind • Layla • Night Moves • Yesterday.
00699569 Book/CD Pack......................................$12.95

VOLUME 3 – HARD ROCK
Crazy Train • Iron Man • Living After Midnight • Rock You like a Hurricane • Round and Round • Smoke on the Water • Sweet Child O' Mine • You Really Got Me.
00699573 Book/CD Pack......................................$14.95

VOLUME 4 – POP/ROCK
Breakdown • Crazy Little Thing Called Love • Hit Me with Your Best Shot • I Want You to Want Me • Lights • R.O.C.K. in the U.S.A. (A Salute to 60's Rock) • Summer of '69 • What I like About You.
_____00699571 Book/CD Pack..........................$12.95

VOLUME 5 – MODERN ROCK
Aerials • Alive • Bother • Chop Suey! • Control • Last Resort • Take a Look Around (Theme from "M:I-2") • Wish You Were Here.
_____00699574 Book/CD Pack..........................$12.95

VOLUME 6 – '90S ROCK
Are You Gonna Go My Way • Come Out and Play • I'll Stick Around • Know Your Enemy • Man in the Box • Outshined • Smells like Teen Spirit • Under the Bridge.
_____00699572 Book/CD Pack..........................$12.95

VOLUME 7 – BLUES GUITAR
All Your Love (I Miss Loving) • Born Under a Bad Sign • Crosscut Saw • I'm Tore Down • Pride and Joy • The Sky Is Crying • Sweet Home Chicago • The Thrill Is Gone.
_____00699575 Book/CD Pack..........................$12.95

VOLUME 8 – ROCK
All Right Now • Black Magic Woman • Get Back • Hey Joe • Layla • Love Me Two Times • Won't Get Fooled Again • You Really Got Me.
_____00699585 Book/CD Pack..........................$12.95

VOLUME 9 – PUNK ROCK
All the Small Things • Fat Lip • Flavor of the Weak • Hash Pipe • I Feel So • Pretty Fly (For a White Guy) • Say It Ain't So • Self Esteem.
_____00699576 Book/CD Pack..........................$12.95

VOLUME 10 – ACOUSTIC
Have You Ever Really Loved a Woman? • Here Comes the Sun • The Magic Bus • Norwegian Wood (This Bird Has Flown) • Space Oddity • Spanish Caravan • Tangled up in Blue • Tears in Heaven.
_____00699586 Book/CD Pack..........................$12.95

VOLUME 11 – EARLY ROCK
Fun, Fun, Fun • Hound Dog • Louie, Louie • No Particular Place to Go • Oh, Pretty Woman • Rock Around the Clock • Under the Boardwalk • Wild Thing.
_____00699579 Book/CD Pack..........................$12.95

VOLUME 12 – POP/ROCK
Every Breath You Take • I Wish It Would Rain • Money for Nothing • Rebel, Rebel • Run to You • Ticket to Ride • Wonderful Tonight • You Give Love a Bad Name.
_____00699587 Book/CD Pack..........................$12.95

VOLUME 13 – FOLK ROCK
Leaving on a Jet Plane • Suite: Judy Blue Eyes • Take Me Home, Country Roads • This Land Is Your Land • Time in a Bottle • Turn! Turn! Turn! (To Everything There Is a Season) • You've Got a Friend • You've Got to Hide Your Love Away.
_____00699581 Book/CD Pack..........................$12.95

VOLUME 14 – BLUES ROCK
Blue on Black • Crossfire • Cross Road Blues (Crossroads) • The House Is Rockin' • La Grange • Move It on Over • Roadhouse Blues • Statesboro Blues.
_____00699582 Book/CD Pack..........................$12.95

VOLUME 15 – R&B
Ain't Too Proud to Beg • Brick House • Get Ready • I Can't Help Myself (Sugar Pie, Honey Bunch) • I Got You (I Feel Good) • I Heard It Through the Grapevine • My Girl • Shining Star.
_____00699583 Book/CD Pack..........................$12.95

VOLUME 16 – JAZZ
All Blues • Black Orpheus • Bluesette • Footprints • Misty • Satin Doll • Stella by Starlight • Tenor Madness.
_____00699584 Book/CD Pack..........................$12.95

VOLUME 17 – COUNTRY
All My Rowdy Friends Are Coming over Tonight • Amie • Boot Scootin' Boogie • Chattahoochee • Folsom Prison Blues • Friends in Low Places • T-R-O-U-B-L-E • Workin' Man Blues.
_____00699588 Book/CD Pack..........................$12.95

VOLUME 18 – ACOUSTIC ROCK
About a Girl • Breaking the Girl • Drive • Iris • More Than Words • Patience • Silent Lucidity • 3 AM.
_____00699577 Book/CD Pack..........................$12.95

VOLUME 19 – SOUL
Get up (I Feel like Being) a Sex Machine • Green Onions • In the Midnight Hour • Knock on Wood • Mustang Sally • (Sittin' On) the Dock of the Bay • Soul Man • Walkin' the Dog.
_____00699578 Book/CD Pack..........................$12.95

VOLUME 20 – ROCKABILLY
Blue Suede Shoes • Bluejean Bop • Hello Mary Lou • Little Sister • Mystery Train • Rock This Town • Stray Cat Strut • That'll Be the Day.
_____00699580 Book/CD Pack..........................$12.95

Prices, contents, and availability subject to change without notice.

FOR MORE INFORMATION, SEE YOUR LOCAL MUSIC DEALER, OR WRITE TO:

7777 W. BLUEMOUND RD. P.O. BOX 13819 MILWAUKEE, WI 53213

Visit Hal Leonard online at www.halleonard.com

GUITAR SONGBOOKS FOR THE HOLIDAYS

   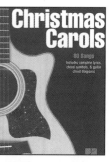  

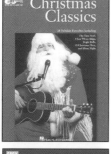   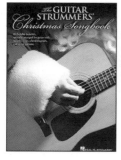 

THE BIG CHRISTMAS COLLECTION FOR EASY GUITAR

Includes over 70 Christmas favorites, such as: Ave Maria • Blue Christmas • Deck the Hall • Feliz Navidad • Frosty the Snow Man • Happy Holiday • A Holly Jolly Christmas • Joy to the World • O Holy Night • Silver and Gold • Suzy Snowflake • You're All I Want for Christmas • and more.
00698978 Easy Guitar with Notes and Tab $16.95   **INCLUDES TAB**

CHRISTMAS CHEER FOR EASY GUITAR

26 songs, including: Blue Christmas • The Christmas Song (Chestnuts Roasting) • Frosty, the Snow Man • Happy Xmas • It's Beginning to Look Like Christmas • Rudolph the Red-Nosed Reindeer • Wonderful Christmastime • and more.
00702048 Easy Guitar with Notes and Tab $10.95   **INCLUDES TAB**

CHRISTMAS CLASSICS

Over 25 easy guitar arrangements of Christmas favorites: Auld Lang Syne • Away in a Manger • Deck the Hall • The First Noel • I Saw Three Ships • Jingle Bells • O Christmas Tree • Once in a Royal David's City • Silent Night • Up on the Housetop • What Child Is This? • and more. Easy guitar arrangements in standard notation and tablature.
00702028 Easy Guitar with Notes and Tab $7.95   **INCLUDES TAB**

CHRISTMAS FAVORITES - 2ND EDITION

A collection of 33 seasonal songs in standard notation and tab. Includes: Angels We Have Heard on High • The First Noel • I Saw Three Ships • Joy to the World • O Come All Ye Faithful • O Holy Night • What Child Is This • and more.
00699097 Easy Guitar with Notes and Tab $9.95   **INCLUDES TAB**

CHRISTMAS TIDINGS

23 easy arrangements of Christmas favorites, including: Blue Christmas • The Chipmunk Song • Feliz Navidad • Grandma Got Run Over by a Reindeer • Happy Holiday • I'll Be Home for Christmas • Rudolph the Red-Nosed Reindeer • Silver Bells • and more.   **INCLUDES TAB**
00699123 Easy Guitar with Notes and Tab $9.95

CONTEMPORARY CHRISTIAN CHRISTMAS

19 contemporary favorites recorded by top artists: Breath of Heaven (Mary's song) • Celebrate the Child • Child of Bethlehem • Emmanuel • Good News • Jesus is Born • One Small Child • Precious Promise • A Strange Way to Save the World • This Gift • This Little Child • and more.
00702170 Easy Guitar with Notes and Tab $9.95   **INCLUDES TAB**

CHRISTMAS CAROLS — GUITAR CHORD SONGBOOK

Includes complete lyrics, chord symbols, and guitar chord diagrams. A convenient reference of 80 Christmas carols for the player who just needs the lyrics and chords. Songs include: Angels We Have Heard on High • Away in a Manger • Deck the Hall • Good King Wenceslas • The Holly and the Ivy • I Heard the Bells on Christmas Day • Jingle Bells • Joy to the World • O Holy Night • Silent Night • Up on the Housetop • We Wish You a Merry Christmas • Welsh Carol • What Child Is This? • and more.
00699536 Guitar Chords/Lyrics $12.95

CHRISTMAS SONGS FOR GUITAR

The Strum It! series lets guitar players strum the chords (and sing along) with their favorite songs. The songs in each book have been selected because they can be played with regular open chords, barre chords, or other moveable chord types. All songs are shown in their original keys complete with chords, strum patterns, melody and lyrics. This book features over 45 Christmas favorites, including: The Christmas Song (Chestnuts Roasting on an Open Fire) • Feliz Navidad • Frosty the Snow Man • Grandma Got Run over by a Reindeer • The Greatest Gift of All • (There's No Place Like) Home for the Holidays • I'll Be Home for Christmas • It's Beginning to Look like Christmas • The Most Wonderful Time of the Year • Rockin' Around the Christmas Tree • Rudolph the Red-Nosed Reindeer • Silver Bells • and more.
00699247 Strum It Guitar $9.95

A FINGERSTYLE GUITAR CHRISTMAS

Over 20 songs for fingerstyle guitar: Auld Lang Syne • Ave Maria • Away in a Manger • The Coventry Carol • Dec.k the Hall • The First Noel • Good King Wenceslas • I Saw Three Ships • Joy to the World • Silent Night • Up on the Housetop • What Child Is This? • and more.
00699038 Fingerstyle Guitar $12.95   **INCLUDES TAB**

THE GUITAR STRUMMER'S CHRISTMAS SONGBOOK

A great collection of 80 favorite Christmas tunes that can be played with open chords, barre chords or other moveable chord types - all in their original keys, complete with chords, strum patterns, melody and lyrics. Includes: The Christmas Song (Chestnuts Roasting on an Open Fire) • Christmas Time Is Here • Do They Know It's Christmas? • Feliz Navidad • Frosty the Snow Man • Grandma Got Run over by a Reindeer • A Holly Jolly Christmas • I Heard the Bells on Christmas Day • I've Got My Love to Keep Me Warm • It's Christmas in New York • Let It Snow! Let It Snow! Let It Snow! • My Favorite Things • O Holy Night • Rudolph the Red-Nosed Reindeer • Silver Bells • We Wish You a Merry Christmas • You Make It Feel like Christmas • and more.
00699527 Melody/Lyrics/Chords $14.95

HAPPY HOLIDAY

20 holiday favorites arranged for fingerstyle guitar, including: Happy Holiday • I'll Be Home for Christmas • My Favorite Things • Rockin' Around the Christmas Tree • Silver Bells • and more.
00699209 Fingerstyle Guitar $10.95   **INCLUDES TAB**

LET IT SNOW!

22 songs for fingerstyle guitar, including: Blue Christmas • The Christmas Song (Chestnuts Roasting on an Open Fire) • Feliz Navidad • Frosty the Snow Man • Jingle-Bell Rock • We Need a Little Christmas • and more.
00699206 Fingerstyle Guitar $10.95   **INCLUDES TAB**

Prices, contents, and availability subject to change without notice.

FOR MORE INFORMATION, SEE YOUR LOCAL MUSIC DEALER, OR WRITE TO:

HAL•LEONARD®
CORPORATION

7777 W. BLUEMOUND RD. P.O. BOX 13819 MILWAUKEE, WI 53213

www.halleonard.com

0703